Contents

Introduction 5

Surfing 9

Getting started 17

Who can become a surfer? 22

Who are the professional surfers? 31

Competing in surfing 35

Quick facts about surfing 42

Glossary 44

Internet sites and addresses 46

Books and magazines 47

Index 48

Safe surfers have respect for the ocean in which they ride their boards.

Surfing

Chuck Miller

Raintree

www.raintreepublishers.co.uk

Visit our website to find out more information about **Raintree** books.

To order:
☎ Phone 44 (0) 1865 888112
🖹 Send a fax to 44 (0) 1865 314091
💻 Visit the Raintree Bookshop at www.raintreepublishers.co.uk to browse our catalogue and order online.

First published in Great Britain by Raintree Publishers, Halley Court, Jordan Hill, Oxford, OX2 8EJ, part of Harcourt Education.
Raintree is a registered trademark of Harcourt Education Ltd.

©Harcourt Education Ltd 2003
First Published in paperback in 2004
The moral right of the proprietor has been asserted.

Consultant: Meg Bernardo, Surfing America

Editor: Isabel Thomas
Cover Design: Michelle Lisseter
Production: Jonathan Smith

Originated by Dot Gradations Ltd
Printed and bound in China and Hong Kong by South China

ISBN 1 844 21289 0 (hardback)
07 06 05 04 03
10 9 8 7 6 5 4 3 2 1

ISBN 1 844 21294 7 (paperback)
08 07 06 05 04
10 9 8 7 6 5 4 3 2 1

British Library Cataloguing in Publication Data
A catalogue for this book is available from the British Library

Acknowledgements
The publishers would like to thank the following for permission to reproduce photographs:
Steve Ryan: pp. **1, 15, 16, 18, 20, 28. 30, 32–33, 34, 39, 42 top**; Heather Holjes: pp. **6, 24, 26, 36, 40, 43 top and bottom**; Klein: pp. **8, 12, 42** bottom; Corbis pp. **4–5, 22–23**

Cover photograph reproduced with permission of Sporting Pictures.

Every effort has been made to contact copyright holders of any material reproduced in this book. Any omissions will be rectified in subsequent printings if notice is given to the publishers.

Introduction

Extreme sports are relatively new sports taken up
by daring athletes. They are fun, but can also be
dangerous. People who take part in extreme sports
must do everything they can to be safe and avoid
injuries. Surfing is one of the oldest extreme sports,
but is growing more and more popular. Surfers ride
special boards on **ocean** waves. Some ride inside
waves, in what is called the **tube**.

You have probably seen surfers on television or at
the beach. But do you know what a **bodyboard** is? Do
you know the difference between a **long board** and a
short board or how surfing began? Who are the top
surfers in the world today? What do you need to do if
you want to take up surfing? This book will answer all
of these questions and more.

Surfers can have fun on any size of wave.

How to use this book

This book is divided into parts called chapters. The title of each chapter tells you what it is about. The table of contents on page 3 is a list of chapters and their page numbers. The index on page 48 gives you more page numbers where you can find out about the main topics discussed in this book.

Each chapter has colourful photographs, captions and information boxes. The photographs show you some of the things written about in the book. A caption is an explanation that tells you more about a photograph. The captions in this book are in pale blue boxes. Special boxes give you extra information about the subject.

You may not know what some of the words in this book mean. To learn new words, you should look them up in a dictionary. This book has a small dictionary called a glossary. Words that appear in **bold** type are explained in the glossary on page 44.

▲ Most experienced surfers are always on the
  lookout for big waves like this one.

You can use the Internet sites listed on page 46 to
learn more about topics discussed in this book. You
could write letters to the addresses of organizations
listed on page 46, asking them questions or asking
them to send you helpful information.

Surfing

Surfers ride their boards across ocean waves. They ride close to the beach because the best waves are found here. Most surfers ride in the Atlantic and Pacific oceans, especially near **Hawaii**. They look for places with large waves that allow them to do tricks. Tricks can be done on waves or in the air above them.

Surfers need to be in good shape to surf safely. They have to know the area where they surf. They should not surf in water that is not deep enough. They could hit the bottom of the ocean if they fell off their boards in shallow water.

Surfers should not surf in the part of the ocean that boats use. This is not safe for surfers or boaters. Surfers should not surf in water where **sharks** have been seen.

Surfing safely

Surfers need to be strong swimmers. Their boards may get washed away from them when they fall off. They should be able to swim all the way back to the beach.

Surfers should never ride alone. Friends can find help for a surfer who needs it. Young people must never ride without an adult nearby.

Rough play is not allowed when surfing. Surfers should never try to knock each other off their boards. They should never bump into each other. Surfers who do this could injure or even kill someone. An injury is some kind of hurt or damage, like a broken bone or a sprain. A sprain means that one of the body's joints has been twisted, tearing its muscles or ligaments. Ligaments hold together the bones in a joint.

Different types of surfing

Most extreme surfers use **short boards**. Short boards are about 2 metres long. They are easy to steer and surfers can do difficult tricks on them.

Less experienced surfers use **long boards**, which are about 2.5 metres to more than 3 metres long. These boards are hard to turn quickly, but they float well on large waves.

Some surfers ride tandem on long boards. This means that two surfers ride on the same board. This is difficult to do. The surfers must work as a team to turn and do tricks.

Other surfers ride **bodyboards**. These are even shorter than short boards. Surfers lie down on their stomachs to ride them.

Surfing timeline

1778: Captain James Cook sees surfers in the Hawaiian islands

1912: Duke Kahanamoku surfs near the California shore

1935: Tom Blake puts a fin on his surfboard

1930s: Surfboard makers begin making lighter boards

1978: National Scholastic Surfing Association begins teaching surfing

This surfer is riding inside the wave's tube.

The big wave

The wind makes waves by stirring up ocean water near the shore. Most surfers try to ride the tallest waves they can find. These are often shaped like a tube. They become tube-shaped when the water at the top of the wave curls over the water at the bottom of the wave and there is space for air in between. Extreme surfers can do many tricks on these waves. But these waves can be dangerous.

Beginners should not ride the tallest waves they can find. They should ride smaller ones that are no taller than they are. These are easier and safer to ride.

Boarder profile: Duke Kahanamoku

Duke Kahanamoku is often called the father of modern surfing. He was born in Hawaii in 1890. In 1912, he won an Olympic gold medal in swimming. He also began travelling the world to show people how to surf. People thought that his long, heavy wooden surfboard looked strange, until he showed them how he could use it to ride waves. Kahanamoku died in 1968, but his name lives on among surfers. In 1999, *Surfer* magazine put Kahanamoku on its cover. It said he was the best surfer of the century.

How surfing began

Surfing began more than 1000 years ago in the southern regions of the Pacific Ocean. People who lived on the islands that are now called Hawaii were the first surfers. They used boards made from wood. These were solid and heavy.

In 1778, a British explorer called James Cook sailed to Hawaii. He landed in Kealakekua Bay, where he saw that the people were good surfers. He noticed that almost all the men surfed.

In 1912, a Hawaiian man called Duke Paoa Kahanamoku visited California in the USA. He was a good swimmer and surfer. He surfed at many spots in the Pacific Ocean near Californian shores. People who watched him often wanted to start surfing too. But his boards were long, heavy and difficult to steer.

Surfboard makers began making shorter, lighter boards in the 1930s and 1940s. More people began using them to learn how to surf.

Over time, surfboards have changed in shape and size.

In the 1960s, people in the USA started to form surfing groups. A group called the International Surfing Association (ISA) begain to hold surfing competitions around the world. The ISA also makes rules for surfers. Organizations in other countries have their own rules.

This surfer is rubbing special wax on to his board to make it easier to ride.

Getting started

Surfers often wear special suits called **wet suits** to keep themselves warm. Water gets into these tight suits. The surfers' body heat warms the water and stops them from getting too cold.

Surfers usually wear **safety leashes**. One end of a safety leash is tied around the surfer's ankle. The other end is joined to the back of the surfboard. The leash stops the board from hitting other people if the surfer falls off.

Surfers rub a special **wax** onto their boards. This wax goes on the top of the boards so the surfer's feet stick to it better. This stops them from falling off so easily.

Most surfers wear some type of **sunscreen** lotion. This protects their skin from getting burnt by the sun.

▲ Beginners often wear helmets so their heads do not get hurt by their boards.

Surfboards

Surfboards were once made of heavy, solid wood. It took as many as three people to carry one board. Most surfboards today are made of a material called foam. One person can carry a board easily.

Most new surfers use **long boards**. They are slower and more difficult to turn than **short boards**,

18

but they are easier to stay on. New surfers use boards that are thick, wide and only slightly taller than they are. The average starter board is about 7.5 centimetres thick and 55 centimetres wide.

Many surfers who have surfed for a long time use short boards instead. These are more difficult to ride and are not as easy to stay on. They are faster though, and they also turn more quickly. Surfers can do more difficult tricks on them.

Original Hawaiian surfboards

Hawaiians once thought surfboards were very special. They used the wood from only three kinds of tree to make them. The makers dug a hole near the tree they were planning to use. They buried fish in the hole as a gift to their gods so the gods would not mind them taking the tree. Then they cut down the tree with a stone axe.

Making the boards was a tough job. Makers used stone axes to shape trees into surfboards. They pulled the boards down to the beach to finish them. They used axes to make the boards smooth and they coloured them with plant roots. They used oil from nuts to make the surfboards waterproof.

Modern surfboards are not made from trees on the beach. They are made from foam and fibreglass and sold in shops.

Surfboards then and now

The first Hawaiian surfboards were long and heavy. They were often more than 6 metres long and weighed over 70 kilograms.

In 1926, a surfer called Tom Blake made some smaller, lighter boards. People found it easier to ride on his boards. They could also ride waves faster and surfing became more exciting.

In 1935, Blake put a fin on the bottom of his surfboard. It looked like an upside-down shark fin and made his surfboard easier to turn. Today, most surfboards have three fins underneath them.

In the 1940s, surfboard makers started making modern boards from foam and fine threads of glass called fibreglass. The foam is like a tough sponge. Makers shape it and cover it with fibreglass to make it strong and waterproof. These boards are light and easy to ride and turn. Surfers prefer this kind of board.

Who can become a surfer?

Almost anyone can start surfing if they prepare properly. It is important to be physically fit and a strong swimmer. Before starting, you need to get a surfboard and learn the safety rules.

Surfing uses many muscles in the body, so warming up is important. Surfers who warm up their muscles get injured less often and feel more relaxed and awake

while surfing. You should stretch your arms, legs and back muscles before surfing.

All surfers ride with their feet a little wider apart than their shoulders. They point their toes towards the front of the surfboard. Most surfers will lead with their left foot while riding waves. Some lead with their right foot. This is called riding **goofy-footed**.

Surfers must be strong swimmers. Many of them have known how to swim for a long time. Usually, they have taken swimming lessons.

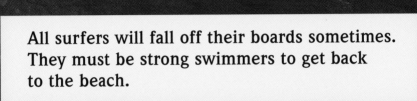

All surfers will fall off their boards sometimes. They must be strong swimmers to get back to the beach.

Surfers learn how to steer their boards across waves by leaning in a certain direction.

Paddling into position

Paddling out into the ocean takes strong muscles. You should lie on your stomach on top of your board and paddle with your arms. You will have to paddle through waves that are already rolling in. One way to stop yourself from being pushed back to the beach is by doing a **push-up**. To do this, hold on to the sides of the board and push your body up by straightening your arms. The wave can then flow around you. You can keep paddling after the wave has passed.

When you see a wave you want to ride, turn your board around and start paddling towards the beach. You have to quickly stand up on your board when the wave is about 3 to 5 metres behind you. When the wave reaches and lifts the board, you will be surfing.

Boarder profile: Mark Occhilupo

Mark Occhilupo surfs on the Association of Surfing Professionals (ASP) World Tour. He is from Australia. He started on the ASP World Tour in 1984. He stopped surfing in 1988, but returned to the sport in 1995. In 1999, he won the ASP championship.

Surfers who have learned how to fall properly are not afraid to fall.

Turning and falling

When you are paddling to catch a wave you should point your board in the direction the wave is moving. This lets you ride the wave longer.

You can turn your board by leaning. Turn right by leaning forwards and turn left by leaning backwards. For people who ride goofy-footed, it is the opposite. You can also learn different ways to turn after you have practised leaning turns.

New surfers often fall down as soon as they catch their first wave. Even professional surfers fall down when they ride tall waves or do difficult tricks. It is important to learn how to fall in the right way. You should try to hold on to your board as you fall. If you cannot hold on, try to fall backwards or to the side of the board. As you go under the water, feel for the pull of your safety leash on your ankle. If you do not feel a pull, cover your head with your hands. This protects your head if the board is right above you.

These beginners are taking lessons from experienced surfing teachers.

Where do I train?

Beginners should take lessons from a surfing instructor who will teach the rules and techniques of surfing quickly. An instructor can also show new surfers what to wear and how to use a safety leash.

Organizations like the British Surfing Association (BSA) and Surfing Australia can help beginners find a surfing instructor. They can give you a list of approved schools so that you can find a instructor in your area.

Surfing is fun to learn, but although it takes just a few weeks to learn the basics, it can take months and years of practise to get good. One of the best ways to learn is to watch other experienced surfers and copy their style.

It is important to know the beach where you surf, so you can avoid rocks and strong currents. Beginners get tired very quickly. You should always return to land as soon as you feel tired.

Did you know?

Did you know that in the past not everyone was allowed to surf? In ancient Hawaii, only kings could surf at some beaches. If ordinary people surfed there, they could be put to death. In surfing competitions, Hawaiian kings sometimes bet their kingdoms on the result.

The best surfers in the world know that it is important to stretch their muscles before surfing ocean waves.

Who are the professional surfers?

Professional, or pro, surfers are people who earn money from surfing. Most pro surfers belong to the Association of Surfing Professionals (ASP). This group holds competitions for **short boards** and **long boards** all year round. Surfers earn points on the World Championship Tour. The surfer who has earned the most points at the end of the year is the champion.

More than 200 international surfers take part in the Salomon Masters at Margaret River in Australia. More than 700 professional surfers ride their boards in the US Open of Surfing. This is the largest surfing competition in the world.

Riding the big waves

Most pro surfers ride the tallest waves they can find. These waves often form **tubes** as they move towards the beach. Surfers try to ride inside the wave tube while doing tricks.

Surfers can also choose to ride the tops of tall waves. Surfers may point the front of their boards off the front of the wave. They can do spins and turns in the air to get back on to the wave.

Surfers will often ride all over a tall wave. They might ride up the front of it and over the top. Then they can turn around and ride back down it. Good surfers can then move straight on to the next wave.

This is professional surfer Brenden Margieson, one of the top surfers in the world.

From this tower, judges can watch and score a surfing competition.

Competing in surfing

Judges give surfers points for the number of tricks they do. Harder tricks earn more points. Surfers are also judged on how original their style is and on the type of waves they ride. The surfer with the highest score wins.

Surfers who ride waves smoothly score higher than those who do not. Surfers who fall off their boards earn no points.

Boarder profile: Sunny Garcia

Sunny Garcia is one of the best pro surfers in the world. He was the 2000 ASP men's world champion. He finished the year ranked first among all male surfers. He was born in Hawaii in 1970 and still lives there. He has been surfing professionally since the 1980s.

This is professional surfer Layne Beachley leaving the ocean after riding waves.

Surfers who ride taller waves may earn more points than those who do not. It is more difficult to do tricks on these waves. Judges give extra points to surfers who ride inside a tall wave's **tube.**

The top surfers in each competition earn prize money. As the men's ASP World Champion in 2000, surfer Sunny Garcia earned nearly £84,000 in prize money. In fifteen years of surfing, he has earned more than £500,000 on the ASP's World Tour.

Boarder Profile: Layne Beachley

Layne Beachley is one of the best female professional surfers in the world. She was the 2000 ASP women's world champion, finishing the year ranked first among all women surfers. She did this three years in a row, winning in 1998, 1999 and 2000. She was born in 1972, in Sydney, Australia, where she says she 'grew up as one of the boys on Manly Beach'. She began competing in surfing events when she was fifteen and turned professional at age seventeen, when she left school.

Sponsors

Professional surfers earn their living from surfing. They enter many events and also travel a lot. This is expensive. Most surfers could not do it without **sponsors**. A sponsor is a company that pays a surfer to use or advertise what it sells.

One well-known sponsor is Oakley. This sunglasses maker sponsors pro surfer Layne Beachley. Oakley pays her to wear its sunglasses while she is on the ASP World Tour. They hope that people who come to watch Layne Beachley surf will want to buy the same sunglasses as their hero.

Boarder profile: Brenden Margieson

Brenden Margieson does not win many competitions on the ASP World Tour, but he is one of the world's top surfers. The ASP has named him the best free surfer in the world twice.

Professional surfers like this one get points for riding difficult waves.

This is Layne Beachley doing a trick on top of a wave.

Competitions and prizes

Every country has its own surfing competitions at all levels. Experienced surfers can start competing with surfers from other countries. The ISA holds the World Surfing Games every two years. Surfers from more than thirty countries enter this competition. They must be members of their country's national team.

Pro surfers from around the world surf on the ASP's World Tour. They try to win prizes and money in competitions.

The number of surfers and competitions around the world continues to grow each year. If you want to take up this sport, get help and advice from experienced surfers first. Joining surf clubs and reading surfing books or magazines will also help you learn more about the sport. Use the pages at the back of this book to get you started.

Did you know?

Do you know who some of the top bodyboarders are? The Australian Michael Eppelstun is one of the top ten bodyboarders in the world. In 1993 he won the Bodyboarding World Title in Hawaii. He finished first, beating Mike Stewart. Stewart had won the world title for eight years in a row before then.

Quick facts about
Surfing

- Some surfers like to ride very tall waves. Jet skis or boats pull them far out into the ocean. Then the surfers ride the waves all the way back to the beach.

- Some surfers like to windsurf. They use a special kind of surfboard with a sail attached to it. Wind catches the sail and pulls the surfer along much faster than they could go on a normal board.

- Great white sharks live in the ocean near Australia and New Zealand. Great whites sometimes attack surfers.

- White water that gently flows on to the beach is called **soup** by surfers.

- To surfers, **wipeouts** are when they fall off their boards.

- Some of the tallest waves in the world are found off the islands of Hawaii.

- Hawaiians invented both surfing and bodyboarding.

Glossary

bodyboard very short surfboard ridden while lying
  face down
goofy-footed riding a board with the right foot
  forwards, instead of the more usual method with the
  left foot forwards
Hawaii group of islands in the Pacific Ocean that make
  up a state in the USA
long board longer surfboard that is easy to ride
  on waves and is used by beginners
ocean huge body of salt water that covers about
  70 per cent of the Earth's surface
professional person who makes money doing something
  amateurs do for fun
push-up where a paddling surfer pushes their body up
  to allow the white water of a broken wave to pass
  between them and their board, so they do not get
  washed back to the beach

safety leash strap that goes around a surfer's ankle and also ties to the surfer's board

shark large fish that feeds on meat and has very sharp teeth

short board shorter surfboard that is easy to turn and do tricks on, used by experienced surfers

soup the white water of a broken wave

sponsor company that pays someone to use what it sells or to advertise its product

sunscreen lotion that protects skin from being burnt by the sun

tube long, hollow area often formed by tall waves

wax substance rubbed on to surfboards to make them stickier and easier to ride

wet suit special suit that uses body heat to warm water to keep a person warm in the sea

wipeout when a surfer falls off their surfboard

Internet sites and addresses

Association of Surfing Professionals
www.aspworldtour.com

British Surfing Association
Champions Yard
Penzance
Cornwall, TR18 2TA
www.britsurf.co.uk

National Surfing Centre
www.nationalsurfingcentre.co.uk

Welsh Surfing Federation
Hillend Campsite
Llangennith
North Gower
Swansea, SA3 1HU
www.welshsurfingfederation.co.uk

Surfing Australia
PO Box 1055
Burleigh Heads
Queensland, QLD 4220
www.surfingaustralia.com

Books and magazines

Radical sports: Surfing, Bizley, Kirk. Heinemann Library, Oxford, 1999

Surf Europe Magazine
Surfing news from Europe and around the world.

Surfer Magazine
Long-running Californian surfing magazine with news, features, photos and product reviews from around the world. See their website www.surfermag.com for more details.

Surfing Magazine
UK magazine with the main news and features available on the website www.surfingthemag.com

Index

Atlantic Ocean 9

Blake, Tom 11, 21
bodyboard 5, 11, 41, 43

Cook, James 11, 14

fibreglass 21
fin 11, 21
foam 18, 21

Hawaii 9, 11, 13, 14, 19,
    21, 29, 35, 41, 43
helmet 18

Kealakekua Bay, Hawaii 14

long board 5, 11, 18

ocean 5, 9, 13, 14, 25, 42

Pacific Ocean 9, 14
paddling 25
professional 25, 31, 32,
    35, 37, 38, 41

safety leash 17, 27, 29
shark 9, 42
short board 5, 11, 18, 19
sponsor 38
sunscreen 17

tandem 11
tube 5, 13, 32, 37

wax 17
wet suit 17